A Note to Parents

DK READERS is a compelling program for beginning readers, designed in conjunction with leading literacy experts, including Dr. Linda Gambrell, Professor of Education at Clemson University. Dr. Gambrell has served as President of the National Reading Conference and the College Reading Association, and has recently been elected to serve as President of the International Reading Association.

Beautiful illustrations and superb full-color photographs combine with engaging, easy-to-read stories to offer a fresh approach to each subject in the series. Each DK READER is guaranteed to capture a child's interest while developing his or her reading skills, general knowledge, and love of reading.

The five levels of DK READERS are aimed at different reading abilities, enabling you to choose the books that are exactly right for your child:

Pre-level 1: Learning to read
Level 1: Beginning to read
Level 2: Beginning to read alone
Level 3: Reading alone
Level 4: Proficient readers

The "normal" age at which a child begins to read can be anywhere from three to eight years old. Adult participation through the lower levels is very helpful for providing encouragement, discussing storylines, and sounding out unfamiliar words.

No matter which level you select, you can be sure that you are helping your child learn to read, then read to learn!

LONDON, NEW YORK, MUNICH,
MELBOURNE, and DELHI

Editorial Lead Heather Jones
Special Sales Production Manager
Silvia La Greca
Associate Publisher Nigel Duffield

Reading Consultant
Linda Gambrell, Ph.D.

Produced by
Shoreline Publishing Group LLC
President James Buckley, Jr.
Designer Tom Carling, carlingdesign.com

The Boy Scouts of America®, Cub Scouts®,
Boys' Life®, and rank insignia are registered
trademarks of the Boy Scouts of America.
Printed under license from the
Boy Scouts of America.

First American Edition, 2008
08 09 10 11 10 9 8 7 6 5 4 3 2 1
Published in the United States by DK Publishing
375 Hudson Street, New York, New York 10014

Published in Great Britain by Dorling Kindersley Limited

DK books are available at special discounts when purchased in bulk
for sales promotions, premiums, fund-raising, or educational use.
For details, contact:
DK Publishing Special Markets, 375 Hudson St., New York, NY 10014
SpecialSales@dk.com

A catalog record for this book is available
from the Library of Congress.
ISBN: 978-0756-637163 (Paperback)

Printed and bound in China by L. Rex Printing Co. Ltd.

Special thanks to fishing expert Gene Kelley,
who has taught fish a thing or two in his time.

The publisher would like to thank the following for their kind
permission to reproduce their photographs:
(Key: a=above; b=below/bottom; c=center; l=left; r=right; t=top)
Corbis: 40, 42, 43; Dreamstime.com (photographers listed): Paul Moore 4, Karin
Lau 7, Nikolay Dimitrov 11, Dewitt 17, Phil Date 23, Rimantas Abromas 26,
Milan Kopcok, Richard Gunion 44, Donna Cuic 45. iStock: 5, 10, 16, 20, 27, 28,
30, 31, 34, 35, 36; Photos.com: 24, 33; Shoreline Publishing Group: 6, 37.
All other images © Dorling Kindersley Limited. For more information
see: www.dkimages.com

Discover more at
www.dk.com

Contents

Boys' Life SERIES

Let's Go

Fishing!

Written by K. C. Kelley

DK Publishing

Let's go fishing!

Time for a quiz: Which of these activities attracts the most people each year: playing baseball, playing basketball, or fishing?

If you answered fishing, you're right—and you might *be* one of those people!

Going fishing is a great way to spend time with friends. You get to be outdoors, to enjoy the beautiful scenery, and to match wits with fish! Once you start fishing, you might never stop.

Many people start fishing as kids and make it their lifelong hobby. This book will give you the basics so you can get started. You'll learn about fishing gear and where to find fish. But you'll find that part of the fun of fishing is learning more about it from friends and family.

Fishing is an easy hobby to enjoy. To get started, you just need a few pieces of gear. We'll tell you a little bit about that in the next chapters. You also need to find a place to fish. Your local parks department can help you find some areas near you that are safe to fish. You might fish off of a dock or pier, into

Play by the rules

Make sure to find out about rules in the area where you want to fish. You might need a license to fish in some places. It may not be legal to catch certain fish, or there may be times of year when you can't fish.

FISHING PIER

a pond or lake, or alongside a river. If you live near the ocean, you can go out on a boat to try to catch different kinds of sea life.

Another fun thing about fishing is that some types of fish are really tasty! However, most fishing you do will be "catch and release." That means you hook and land the fish, then carefully remove the hook and release the fish back to the water.

Of course, don't forget to take a picture first!

Tackling tackle

Catching fish is easy, right? You just stick a net in the water and grab them. Well, no, it's not quite that easy. You catch fish by putting a baited hook on a string, or line, into the water. You can also attach a type of hook called a lure to the end of your line.

You hope that the fish will think your bait is something good to eat. Once they bite, the metal hook grabs them, and you can pull them in by reeling in the line the hook is attached to.

Fishing gear is called "tackle." Tackle includes fishing rods, reels, line, and, of course, all those different kinds of bait. We'll talk about bait in a few pages. Right now, let's start with fishing rods.

First, don't call them "poles" if you want people to think you're a real angler (that's a cool name for a person who fishes!). Fishing rods are long, flexible sticks that sometimes come in sections you can assemble. The rod has rings for the line along one side. A handle at the bottom end makes it easier to hold on to. The reel is attached near the bottom, too.

Rings for line

This closeup shows the thin tip and rings (left) and the handle of a typical fishing rod.

A reel is a circular device that holds the line and makes it easy for you to pull in line or let line out. The type of reel you use will depend on the type of fishing you are doing.

With most reels, you will have to learn to cast. Casting means to throw the lure or hook out on the water using the rod. New anglers should practice casting on dry land first.

The black button on this spincasting reel lets line out.

The reel most kids start fishing with is with a spincasting (or baitcasting) reel. This reel is mounted on the top of the fishing rod handle. The reel has a handle on the side that you turn to pull in the line. A button on the reel releases the line as you cast.

Spinning reel

A spinning reel is attached on the underside of the rod's handle. You control how much line goes out with your index finger. Both types of reels have a way to control how quickly the line pulls off the reel. Like raising or lowering a bike seat, adjust this control so that your line pulls off smoothly.

Fishermen collect hooks, lures, and other gear like birds collect sticks for a nest. They just can't get enough! Your gear will fit into a small tackle box. Use a plastic tackle box to prevent rusting.

You'll need hooks of several sizes. Hooks are numbered and the higher the number, the smaller the hook. You can also try hooks without "barbs." Hooks without these sharp points are safer and easier to remove from the fish.

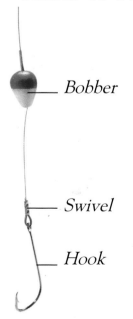

Bobber

Swivel

Hook

To keep the bait or lures from floating, use sinkers. These small weights attach to the line and help get the bait sink. Bobbers can be used to help you keep track of where your bait is.

Swivels attach above the

Anglers love fishing gear almost as much as they love fishing!

hook and keep your line and lures from becoming tangled.

So, putting it all together, at the end of your line, you'll attach a lure or a hook for bait, a sinker, and a swivel.

Now it's time to feed some fish. Feed them? Weren't we going to catch them? Well, to catch them, you first have to convince them to eat.

Think like a fish

To catch fish, you have to think like a fish . . . a hungry fish. The things you put in the water to catch fish need to be attractive to fish. That is, you have to convince the fish that your bait or lure is really a tasty treat.

Most likely, the fish you'll be trying to catch will like to eat live prey. So the easiest type of bait to use is live bait—such as worms.

Now, some kids think this is kind of gross. You take a wiggly worm and put it on a hook and toss it in the water. Bad news for the worm, but good news for a hungry fish. The worms move around underwater and attract fish. You can also use small live fish.

If you don't want to use live bait, you can put chunks of cut-up fish on your hook as well. It won't move like live bait, but it will have a good, fishy smell and taste, especially if it's fresh.

In "catch and release" fishing, carefuly remove the hook after you land the fish.

Many fishermen try to fool their fish by using lures. Lures are designed to imitate the look and movement of fish or insects that other fish would like to eat. The lures have hooks, too, so that when the fish bites what they think is lunch—you've got 'em!

There are as many types and designs of lures as there are types of fish. Some lures are big and flashy, others are small and sleek. You'll see lures with bright colors like blues and reds and others with softer colors like greens and browns.

Different lures will attract different types of fish. Check with local experts to find out which types of lures work in the fishing areas you'll be using. But be polite about asking—some fishemen like to keep their secrets . . . secret!

One special way to fool fish is by using flies. Not real houseflies, however. In fishing, flies are hooks covered with everything from feathers and fur to fuzz and scales. The flies are carefully tied to make them look as much like tasty insects as possible. If a fish sees the "insect," it will strike!

Tying flies is a whole other part of fishing and one that you might enjoy learning about from an expert. Even if you don't tie your own flies, there are many available for you to try out.

Flies like those opposite are "tied" as shown above.

Your tackle box will hold all your hooks, lures, line, sinkers, and similar small items. Along with all that, however, you should consider taking a few other items when you go fishing.

You'll be near water, so you should have a flotation device such as a life vest. A bucket is great for carrying your gear, plus it makes a handy stool to sit on while you fish.

A pair of needle-nose pliers are very useful, too. They are a good and safe way to help remove hooks from a fish's mouth. Don't forget fingernail clippers. They're not for your fingers—they're a quick and easy way to snip extra fishing line.

Needle-nose pliers

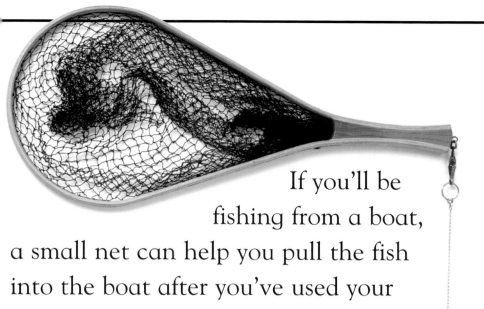

If you'll be
fishing from a boat,
a small net can help you pull the fish
into the boat after you've used your
reel to bring them close.

Some busy anglers wear a vest
with several pockets that can hold
other little things that they might need
while they're fishing.

Fishing safety tips
1. Wear a flotation device whenever you're on a boat
   or fishing alongside water.
2. Always be aware of those around you. Those hooks
   are sharp and you want to catch fish, not a friend!
3. Wear sunscreen!
4. Bring dry clothing to change into if you'll be
   getting wet while fishing.

Freshwater fishing

Now, with all your gear in hand—let's find the fish! Most of you will fish in freshwater. That means ponds, lakes, rivers, or streams.

But where do you put your hook? You can't see the fish in the water (usually), so how do you know where they are? Time to think like a fish again. You already got into their heads to bring along bait or lures they'd want to eat. Where would a fish like to hang out?

Generally, fish don't like crowds and noise, so try to find quiet spots with few other fishermen. Fish like to be around something else underwater, so look for rocky areas in the water, the weeds along a shore or bank, or a spot of shade created by an overhanging tree.

The most important skill for freshwater fishing is casting. Before you head to the water, you should practice casting (with a small weight but without a hook!) on dry land. Set out a target about 25 feet (7.5 m) away. You can use a soda can or an old hat as targets.

Casting is sort of like throwing a football or a baseball, but without taking a step. Hold the rod with your "throwing" hand. You should face your target and raise the rod tip up by bending

your elbow.
After the rod
is pointing
straight
up or a
little behind you,
quickly bring your
forearm forward, snapping the lure in
the direction of the target.

At the same time, you will be busy
with the reel. With a spinning reel
shown above, hold the line against the
rod as you bring the rod forward. As you
reach out in front of you, lift your finger
to let the line go. On a spincasting reel,
there is a button you hold down and
release as you cast to let the line go.

Casting is like any skill—the more
you practice, the better you'll become.

You can fish in freshwater from the side or bank of a stream, river, or pond. However, on larger bodies of water, such as a lake, you can fish from a boat.

Fishing from a boat has some special challenges, but it can be worth the effort. There's nothing quite as pleasant as sitting on a quietly bobbing boat with your family or friends, just putting a line in the water.

As on any boat, you should not stand up. Even when reeling in a fish, try to remember not to tip the boat. Work with the other people in the boat to keep your lines from tangling, too. If someone is reeling in a fish, reel your line in to stay out of his way.

Always get permission before setting out on any boat trip, and never go out alone. Don't forget your life jacket!

Bassmasters

Pro bass fishermen have become big sports heroes. Their competitions are shown on TV and the winners can earn big prizes. During tournaments, the angler who catches the most fish by weight wins.

Flyfishing

Flyfishing is a very different kind of freshwater fishing. Anglers use longer rods and a special kind of reel. They attach "flies" to their line to attract fish. The two most popular kinds of flies are "wet" and "dry." Wet flies imitate insects in their youngest stage, when they actually live in the water. Dry flies look like adult insects with wings. Each is cast in a different way to help "fool" the fish.

Flyfishing has a long history and is very popular in areas with rivers and streams. Flyfishermen often try to catch sneaky trout, hard-fighting salmon, or smallmouth bass.

Flyfishing reel

Casting with a flyfishing rod is more difficult than with a spincasting rod or spinner. Doing it well takes a lot more practice. The fly is also much lighter than a lure or bait. How the fly is "presented," or shown to the fish is very important. A fly that splashes wrong or doesn't move like the insect it's imitating won't attract fish.

Fly rods are longer than most other rods and the casting motion is much wider and smoother. As soon as you cast the fly, the current will carry it away. You use the slack in the line to "play" the fly. Remember, you're trying to pretend it's an insect. When you get a "hit," you reel it all back in right away.

However, big fans of flyfishing will tell you there's nothing more pleasant than a day on a slowly moving river making cast after cast. Catching the fish is fun, too!

Saltwater fishing

Scientists tell us that 70 percent of the Earth's surface is covered by water—saltwater, that is. That's a lot of space for fish to roam! Going out on the ocean to catch saltwater fish is different than tracking them down on a pond or lake, but it's a fun experience, too.

You can catch some saltwater fish from a pier or dock or even from the shore. It's a lot like freshwater fishing. You need a rod, reel, and bait.

Spincasting or spinning reels can be used to get your bait out where the fish are. Live bait works best for most saltwater fish, though some very large sport fish are caught with big lures. A kind of lure called a "spoon" spins around, flashing silver like a minnow

as you reel it through the water. Some experts use flies to catch other saltwater fish, but it's probably not a good way to go on your first ocean trips.

Anglers aiming for bigger saltwater fish use a special, very large reel. These big devices hold miles and miles of heavy line. They toss out lures and hooks designed to catch fish that can weigh hundreds of pounds.

While some freshwater fish, like bass or salmon, will fight very hard once they're hooked, the big ocean "sportfish" really put up a battle. Giant black marlin or huge sailfish can battle an angler for hours. They might take the boat on a chase that goes on for miles as the fisherman's shoulders and hands ache. The driver of the boat can play a big role in these fights, too, as he steers the boat over the waves after the fish. Experts who reel in these big fish say the battle is worth it, however. That's a fish story to tell for years!

Another fun way to enjoy saltwater fishing is on a group fishing boat. These large boats can carry a couple dozen fishermen and their gear to fishing spots offshore. Most such boats have galleys,

or kitchens, to serve breakfast or lunch during the half-day or day-long trips. The crew will help you find the fish. They'll also advise you about which bait has been working in the area.

A heron waits for someone to drop their bait!

On a fishing boat, find a spot along the rail and cast into the deep water. Because the water is deep, you'll probably release more line and spend more time reeling than with shallow freshwater fishing. But you'll also be trying to catch very different fish! Many saltwater fish make great meals. The boat crew will prepare your fish to take back home for a fresh-caught barbecue!

A fishing trip

Now that you've read about the basics of fishing, let's take a fishing trip and put all your knowledge into action!

Imagine you and your friends are heading out to fish at a nearby lake. You'll be fishing from the bank of the lake, so you won't need a boat or a life preserver. But you will need other fishing gear.

The first step is to find out what kind of fish live in the lake. You can ask at local bait shops or read up on the fish in

guide books about the area. You'll have to make sure that you bring the kind of bait or lures that attract the local types of fish. You can't bring bait for salmon if your lake only has bass!

Once you know what to bring for bait, you can assemble your tackle box. Don't forget extra line, hooks, and sinkers. Bobbers (below right) can be helpful, too. These float on the surface of the water and help the bait "hang" in place for fish to eat.

Rubber boots are great for muddy banks.

Now it's time to head for the lake.
Look around for a good spot to fish
from. Stand away from other fishermen,
if there are any there ahead of you.
A shady spot is a good place to start
making your casts.

Prepare your line by tying on a bobber if you choose to use one; a sinker; a swivel; and then the lure or hook. If you're using a hook, don't forget to put on the bait. Bait might be a worm or a small piece of fish. (We've heard that lake fish sometimes like to eat pieces of ham, too!).

Check carefully around you to make sure the area is clear, then cast your line out onto the water. Depending on the type of reel you're using, you'll either pull the line back in or let it sink.

At this point, you'll learn another important part of fishing: patience. Sometimes it might take hours and dozens of casts (hundreds if you're flyfishing) to get those fish to bite. Don't get discouraged if a fish doesn't snag your hook five minutes after you start fishing. Just wait . . . they'll come.

Watch the tip of your rod carefully, or watch the bobber if you're using one. When they dip or sink suddenly, you might have a bite. When you feel that, pull the rod tip back quickly toward you. This is called "setting the hook." Otherwise, the fish might just spit it out. Once you feel a strong tug on the line, you've got it! Fish on!

Reel the fish in slowly, pulling up on the rod as you do. Soon, you'll be able to proudly hold up your catch!

Wow, what a beauty! You've brought in a brook trout. Look at its shimmering skin! But don't wait very long before releasing the fish back to the water to swim again. Get your hands wet before you handle the fish; this will protect its delicate skin. Then, using the pliers from your tackle box, carefully remove the hook from the fish's mouth.

The fish might be tired from the fight, so try to help it catch its breath. Lower the fish back into the water and wiggle around a bit. Then let it go, and with a flip of its tail, it will head back into the lake. Maybe the two of you will "catch up" again someday!

At the end of your afternoon on the lake, it's time to pack up and go home. Make sure not to leave any hooks, line, or other gear or trash at your fishing site. Take only pictures and leave only footprints!

Fishing with family and friends is a great way to spend a day outdoors. Here's hoping one day you "land a big one!"

Find out more
Books

The Barefoot Fisherman's Guide
by Paul Amdahl
This very fact-filled book covers everything from how to cast different sorts of reels to how to fish for everything from bass to walleye.

How to Catch a Fish
by John Frank
Here's a very unique look at fishing: The author has put together a book of poems on how fishing is done in places around the world. From the Caribbean to Europe to Africa, travel with your imagination (and your fishing rod) as you read these great poems.

Kids' Incredible Fishing Stories
by Shaun Morey
Fishermen are famous for telling "whoppers," or stories about huge fish that "got away." In this book, the author gathers true fish stories from kids. Read about the boy who caught a 1,000-pound shark or the kid who caught a piranha in a lake in Florida!

Web sites

Boys' Life Magazine
www.boyslife.org
The magazine's "Outdoors and Gear" section includes all sorts of tips for fishermen. Meet the Gear Guy, send in your fishing photos, and find new articles on animals, nature, and the outdoors.

Be a fishing winner!
www.kids-fishing.com
Beginning in 2008, visit this site to find out how you can take part in the Kids' All-American Fishing Derby. It's a contest open to any kid who likes to fish.

Get help to go fishing
www.futurefisherman.org
The site of the national organization Future Fishermen offers links to find places near you to fish, fishing techniques, and fishing stories.

Meet a pro!
www.fishnkids.com
Sponsored by a group of pro bass fisherman, this site lets you send questions to the experts about all sorts of fishing.

Note to Parents: These Web sites are not endorsed by Boy Scouts of America or DK Publishing and have not been completely examined. However, at press time, they provided the sort of information described. Internet experts always suggest that you work with your children to help them understand how to safely navigate the Web.

Angler
Another r   a person who fishes. It comes from the angle formed by the fishing rod and the person.

Bait
Fish, insects, or other food material put on a hook to attract fish.

Barbs
Small, sharp points at the end of some fishing hooks.

Cast
Tossing a lure or baited hook into the water by using a fishing rod.

Drag
The speed that a fishing line is pulled out from the reeel; drag can be adjusted to be fast or slow.

imitate living creatures to fool fish into eating them.

Galley
The kitchen on a boat.

Lure
In fishing, a small object designed to attract fish.

Pier
A narrow wood platform sticking out from land into a body of water.

Prey
Animals that other animals hunt and eat.

Reel
A device that holds, releases, and pulls in fishing line when attached to a fishing rod.

pole, with a reel and line, that is used to catch fish.

Sinkers
Small lead weights that help baited hooks or lures go deeper underwater to attract fish.

Sportfish
Large ocean fish such as marlins or sailfish that are popular among deep-sea fishermen.

Swivels
Small devices that are clipped to a fishing line that allow the lure or baited hook to spin freely and easily.

Tackle
Fishing gear.

1998